MCWP 3-33.7

Marine Air-Ground Task Force Combat Camera

US Marine Corps

PCN 143 000105 00

To Our Readers

Changes: Readers of this publication are encouraged to submit suggestions and changes through the Universal Need Statement (UNS) process. The UNS submission process is delineated in Marine Corps Order 3900.15_, *Marine Corps Expeditionary Force Development System*, which can be obtained from the Marine Corps Publications Electronic Library Online (http://www.marines.mil/news/publications/Pages/Publications137.aspx).

The UNS recommendation should include the following information:

- Location of change
    Publication number and title
    Current page number
    Paragraph number (if applicable)
    Line number
    Figure or table number (if applicable)
- Nature of change
    Addition/deletion of text
    Proposed new text

Additional copies: A printed copy of this publication may be obtained from Marine Corps Logistics Base, Albany, GA 31704-5001, by following the instructions in MCBul 5600, *Marine Corps Doctrinal Publications Status*. An electronic copy may be obtained from the MCCDC Doctrine World Wide Web home page: **https://www.doctrine.usmc.mil**.

Unless otherwise stated, whenever the masculine gender is used, both men and women are included.

DEPARTMENT OF THE NAVY
Headquarters United States Marine Corps
Washington, D.C. 20380-1775

19 October 2010

FOREWORD

Marine Corps Warfighting Publication (MCWP) 3-33.7, *Marine Air-Ground Task Force Combat Camera*, informs the Marine air-ground task force (MAGTF) commander and staff planners on combat camera (COMCAM) capabilities. Combat camera is an information resource that provides a timely, accurate, "you-are-there" imagery perspective on military operations. It is essential to internal and external communications. The need for COMCAM capabilities will increase as the Marine Corps reaches Marine families, interacts with domestic and international media, and provides tactical imagery to enhance force protection and situational awareness. To expedite their decisionmaking processes and operational requirements, commanders must have a successful COMCAM program.

Lessons learned during Operation Enduring Freedom prove that COMCAM units are not fully used due to a lack of understanding of the COMCAM mission and capabilities. Therefore, commanders must realize that COMCAM units make a valuable contribution to the MAGTF and the Marine Corps when COMCAM is understood and the COMCAM officer is supported. Combat camera also provides a visual record for high-level briefs and internal and external communications or historical records.

This publication supersedes MCWP 3-33.7, *Combat Camera and Visual Information in Expeditionary Operations*, 1 October 2002.

Reviewed and approved this date.

BY DIRECTION OF THE COMMANDANT OF THE MARINE CORPS

GEORGE J. FLYNN
Lieutenant General, U.S. Marine Corps
Deputy Commandant for Combat Development and Integration

Publication Control Number: 143 000105 00

DISTRIBUTION STATEMENT A: Approved for public release; distribution is unlimited.

Marine Air-Ground Task Force Combat Camera

Table of Contents

Chapter 3. Planning

Chapter 4. Operations

Chapter 5. Systems and Equipment

Appendices

Glossary

References

Chapter 1
Fundamentals

OVERVIEW

Combat camera (COMCAM) is the acquisition and utilization of still and motion imagery in support of operational and planning requirements across the range of military operations and during exercises. Official visual documentation is used for operational and combat support as well as public information purposes. It is an essential visual record of Marine Corps commands throughout significant and often historical events. Therefore, complete access to areas of operations and timely exploitation of collected imagery are keys to COMCAM success.

MISSION

The mission of COMCAM is to provide the President, Secretary of Defense, Chairman of the Joint Chiefs of Staff (CJCS), Military Departments, combatant commanders, and on-scene commander with a directed image capability in support of operational and planning requirements during world crisis, contingencies, exercises, and wartime operations per Marine Corps Order (MCO) 3104.1A, *Marine Corps Combat Camera Program.*

A fundamental tool of commanders and decisionmakers, COMCAM—

- Provides commanders with combat trained documentation teams that are primary suppliers of operational imagery.

- Supports combat, information, humanitarian, special force; intelligence, surveillance and reconnaissance (ISR); engineering; legal; and public affairs (PA) missions.

- Provides valuable imagery at the strategic, operational, and tactical levels of war.

- Speeds decisionmaking and facilitates the execution of missions at lower levels through vertical and horizontal information flow.

POLICY DOCUMENTS

Policy governing the Joint COMCAM Program is found in Department of Defense Instruction (DODI) 5040.04, *Joint Combat Camera (COMCAM) Program*, which—

- Assigns Joint Combat Camera Program responsibilities.
- Updates COMCAM in support of joint, combined, and Service-specific military operations of joint interest.
- Establishes the Joint Combat Camera Planning Group.

Policy governing visual information is found in DODI 5040.02, *Visual Information (VI)*, which—

- Assigns responsibilities for managing the Department of Defense (DOD) visual information resources.
- Establishes the Joint Visual Information Services Distribution Activity and the Defense Visual Information Center and continues establishment of the DOD Visual Information Steering Committee.

FUNCTION

Marine Corps COMCAM teams are organized, trained, and equipped to provide rapid deployment of COMCAM assets in support of exercises, operations, and contingencies that support the operating forces and are available for tasking by—

- The Secretary of Defense, the CJCS, and federal agencies as directed.
- Unified and subunified combatant commanders.
- Joint and combined task force commanders and their staffs.
- Marine Corps component commanders and their staffs.

Challenges faced by commanders on today's battlefield make COMCAM operations more critical and more difficult to execute. Commanders will exploit imagery at various times and from various sources such as ISR, PA, coalition forces, or civilian media.

Therefore, Marine air-ground task force (MAGTF) COMCAM Marines must be prepared to incorporate COMCAM assets into missions across the full range of military operations, and they must be flexible and able to task-organize COMCAM for any size MAGTF and operation.

Combat camera Marines support a commander's situational awareness, information operations (IO), PA, and civil affairs objectives to include ISR, battlefield damage assessment, military deception, legal, and history functions. Combat camera supports the commander's imagery requirements and produces timely products supporting the commander's intent and mission objectives.

COMBAT CAMERA PRODUCTS

Combat camera provides the MAGTF commander with imagery (video and still), graphics, and printing/reproduction capabilities to facilitate his decisionmaking process and, ultimately, mission accomplishment.

Types of COMCAM products are—

- Still photographic imagery (digital and conventional) (see fig. 1-1).
- Motion imagery (video) (see fig. 1-2 on page 1-6).
- Combat lithography, such as flyers, leaflets, orders, or documents (see fig. 1-3 on page 1-7).
- Combat art (see fig. 1-4 on page 1-9).
- Multimedia digital graphics.

    Note: The above types of COMCAM products are hereafter collectively referred to as COMCAM products.

Figure 1-1. Still Photographic Imagery.

Figure 1-2. Motion Imagery (Video).

PRINCIPLES

Marine Corps COMCAM personnel, the MAGTF commander, and small unit leaders must know the principles that guide the planning and execution of COMCAM operations. These principles include the following:

- *Imagery's worth is increased by the number of viewers.* Imagery becomes useful when it is viewed, shared, used, and understood. Acquisition and production must be synchronized with dissemination options and quickly retrievable archives.

- *Several missions can be supported simultaneously.* Understanding strategic, operational, tactical, immediate, and future COMCAM requirements will empower the COMCAM officer to support concurrent missions, often with the same imagery.

- *The COMCAM applications are boundless.* The application of combat camera requires creative thought to enhance the value of COMCAM units and imagery for mission accomplishment.

- *Combat camera personnel must practice and provide security at the source.* This principle means not sharing information inappropriate for release.

Figure 1-3. Combat Lithograph—Reproduction

INFORMATION OPERATIONS
AND COMBAT CAMERA

The imagery captured by COMCAM units can be used to influence information operations and multiple types of other missions, from major combat operations to small wars. The MAGTF COMCAM organizations—

- Maximize support throughout the MAGTF.

- Must be considered throughout all phases of planning and execution.

- Ensure and maintain operations security.

- Obtain and maintain the commander's trust. This involves anticipating requirements and providing COMCAM products in a usable, understandable, relevant, and timely manner. It also involves restricting access to imagery in accordance with the commander's intent.

- Support DOD and joint COMCAM operations and organizations, including augmenting a joint/combined COMCAM management team.

- Provide camera skills sustainment training for ISR Marines.

- Provide technical advice and guidance on equipment to PA and ISR personnel.

Figure 1-4. Combat Art.

ARCHIVING

The Marine Corps Combat Camera Management Support Center at the Marine Corps Combat Development Command (MCCDC), Quantico, VA, archives COMCAM products forwarded by COMCAM personnel. Imagery, which may have a broader significance to the history of the United States, is submitted to the Defense Imagery Management Operations Center (DIMOC) at the Pentagon. From there, it is available to the general public.

Chapter 2
Organizations and Responsibilities

COMBAT CAMERA PERSONNEL

Occupational field (OccFld) 4600 is comprised of Marines located in COMCAM billets at the—

- Marine Corps forces.
- Marine expeditionary forces (MEFs).
- Marine expeditionary brigades (MEBs).
- Marine expeditionary units (MEUs).
- Ground combat elements (GCEs).
- Aviation combat elements (ACEs).
- Logistics combat elements (LCEs).
- Supporting establishment's base and station COMCAM units and training commands.

The following military occupational specialties (MOSs) comprise OccFld 4600.

4612, Combat Camera Production Specialist, E1 to E6

Combat camera production specialists operate and maintain printing and reproduction equipment. They prepare original layout and design, print multiple formats and sizes, and produce large quantity reproductions.

4616, Reproduction Equipment Repairer Specialist, E4 to E6

Reproduction equipment repairer specialists maintain all tables of equipment (T/E), reproduction-related equipment, and perform administrative and planning functions to include equipment maintenance records.

4641, Combat Photographer, E1 to E6

Combat photographers possess the skill and expertise to document operations in any environment using the latest in still imagery acquisition and production equipment. They are capable and equipped to produce field expedient, still imagery products.

4671, Combat Videographer, E1 to E6

Combat videographers possess the skill and expertise to document operations in any environment using the latest in video imagery acquisition and production equipment. They are capable and equipped to produce field expedient, edited video products.

4691, Combat Camera Chief, E7 to E9

Combat camera chiefs assist the COMCAM officer in supervising, coordinating, administering, and managing COMCAM units and assets. They provide advice and technical expertise to the COMCAM officer and/or MAGTF commander on COMCAM capabilities and deployment and employment of assets.

4602, Combat Camera Officer, Warrant Officer 1 to Major

Combat camera officers supervise, coordinate, administer, and manage COMCAM units and assets. They provide advice and technical expertise to the MAGTF commander on COMCAM capabilities and deployment and employment of COMCAM assets. Officers are an integral part of the planning process, working closely with other staff sections within MAGTF commands to ensure the proper employment of COMCAM and to ensure COMCAM actions and missions support the commander's intent. The COMCAM officer writes appendix 9 (COMCAM) to Annex C (Operations) to the Operation Order (OPORD). See appendix A for additional information.

MARINE CORPS FORCES STAFF

The COMCAM officer develops policy, guidance, and standards for the COMCAM effort throughout the area of operations. The COMCAM officer is the focal point for planning, monitoring, and coordinating COMCAM efforts that support air, ground, and combat service support operations. The COMCAM officer assists the principal staffs and provides guidance to the commander, and specific combatant commander, for all joint exercises, operations, and deployments, requiring COMCAM support. The COMCAM officer is responsible for estimating, recommending, and determining requirements and preparing COMCAM annexes and detailed plans for publication. See appendix B for a sample concept of employment.

MAGTF STAFF

The MAGTF COMCAM officer serves as a battlestaff officer who advises the MAGTF commander on issues, capabilities, and requirements pertaining to COMCAM operations. According to the MCO 3120.10, *Marine Corps Information Operations Program (MCIOP)*, issues, capabilities, and requirements pertaining to COMCAM operations are normally assigned to the assistant chief of staff, operations staff officer (G-3) or the IO cell; the COMCAM officer manages all the MAGTF commander's COMCAM assets to include table of organization and equipment and augmentation tasks from higher command. They task-organize COMCAM personnel for any operational commitments and develop MEF/MEB operational annexes and OPORDs pertaining to COMCAM.

Combat camera personnel are assigned to the MEU command element (CE). Additional assets within the GCE, ACE, and LCE may be tasked to support MEU COMCAM personnel based on operational requirements. Regardless of size, COMCAM units maintain the capability to acquire, edit, disseminate, archive, manage, and transmit imagery. All COMCAM units are equipped to acquire imagery in darkness and inclement weather.

Ground Combat Element

The Marine division's COMCAM unit is the division commander's organic COMCAM capability. Combat camera provides rapid, deployable assets for the execution of operational imagery documentation. The unit supplies task-organized GCEs with COMCAM support to meet the commander's critical information requirements during offensive and defensive operations. This includes direct support to regimental landing teams and battalion landing teams in support of the MAGTF.

Aviation Combat Element

The ACE must be capable of operating from sea-based and shore-based airfields. Operating in a variety of forward-based environments requires a full range of COMCAM capabilities that are organic to the ACE. When an ACE operates from the sea or a forward base, COMCAM is essential to operations. Examples of COMCAM support are site surveys prior to occupation by wing units or targeting folders used to plan strike missions, air assault, or helicopter/parachute landing zones.

Logistics Combat Element

The COMCAM tasks required to support air and ground forces far exceed the organic COMCAM capabilities of the Marine divisions and Marine aircraft wings. All facets of LCE support (such as foreign humanitarian assistance operations and disaster relief) must be documented for historical relevance. Imagery produced by these units has long lasting significance that is vital to lessons learned, training, and future deployments.

SUPPORTING ESTABLISHMENT

Combat camera units exist at major Marine Corps bases and stations and at Headquarters, Marine Corps (HQMC). Each unit is task-organized based on assets available and supports the command's unique mission. Supporting establishment personnel are a vital part of operational sustainment when the requirement for support exceeds the ability of the operational forces' organic assets. Supporting establishment personnel are globally sourced when component commanders identify the need.

Marine Corps base or Marine Corps air station COMCAM units provide support to the supporting establishment and have a dual mission of—

- Providing the means for the Marine Corps to develop, train, and maintain a modern force that is prepared to win the Nation's battles.
- Supporting the quality of life for Marines and their families.

The supporting establishment COMCAM units do not maintain a T/E; therefore, the commander is responsible for equipping and maintaining the centers based on this mission. Commanders must equip Marines with the same systems used in the operating forces. Combat camera offices in HQMC agencies support standardization of COMCAM equipment across the Marine Corps.

Combat camera units should follow guidance set forth in—

- Marine Corps Reference Publication 3-0A, *Unit Training Management Guide*.
- Navy/Marine Corps Departmental Publication (NAVMC) 3500.26, *Combat Camera Training and Readiness Manual.* This publication is used to set up a unit training plan (UTP) to ready supporting establishment COMCAM personnel.

See appendix C for additional information on training.

HEADQUARTERS ELEMENT STAFF

Combat camera personnel in HQMC agencies develop COMCAM warfighting concepts and determine associated required capabilities in the areas of doctrine, organization, training, materiel, leadership and education, personnel, and facilities to enable the Marine Corps to field combat ready COMCAM forces. They also participate in and support other major processes of the Expeditionary Force Development System. Marine Corps Combat Camera Management Support Center is located at Quantico, VA. It is the central point for all imagery archived for Marine Corps COMCAM units.

MAGTF COMMANDER'S RESPONSIBILITIES

The MAGTF commander should ensure that COMCAM assets are tailored to support missions across the full range of military operations. They should also consider imagery requirements that support the Secretary of Defense, Joint Chiefs of Staff, Commandant of the Marine Corps, and all HQMC departments.

Combat camera assets are in all MAGTF elements (see fig. 2-1 on page 2-8). Special requirements may arise where additional personnel are required. The MAGTF commander should request COMCAM personnel augmentation to their unit via higher headquarters CE. The local COMCAM officer will be the action officer for all COMCAM personnel and asset requirements by the commander. The local COMCAM officer will provide personnel and equipment recommendations to the CE staff for approval.

A thorough mission analysis and situational assessment of anticipated COMCAM requirements will assist the higher unit MAGTF commander in deciding how to deploy COMCAM assets. The MAGTF commander should exercise COMCAM capabilities during training exercises, paying particular attention to coordinating with the operational staff, deploying and using all COMCAM functions, and identifying and addressing operations security.

MARINE CORPS
INFORMATION OPERATIONS CENTER

The Marine Corps Information Operations Center (MCIOC) will provide MAGTF commanders and the Marine Corps a responsive and effective full range IO planning and psychological operations (PSYOP) delivery capability by means of deployable support teams and a comprehensive general support IO reachback capability in order to support the integration of IO into Marine Corps operations. This includes, but is not limited to IO subject matter experts in COMCAM.

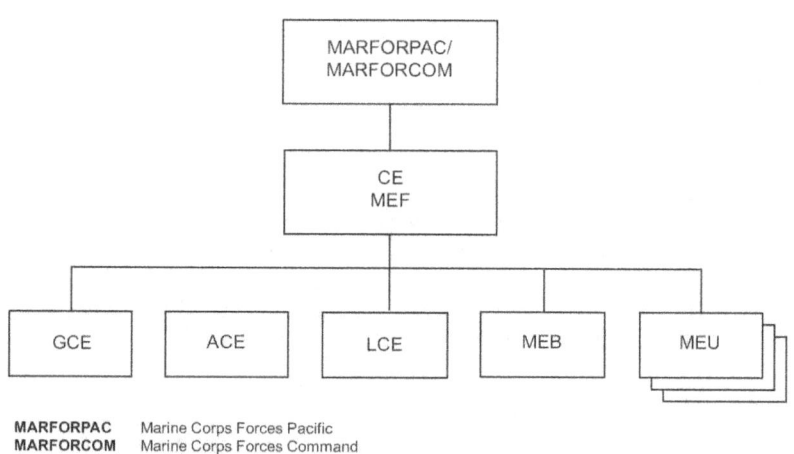

| MARFORPAC | Marine Corps Forces Pacific |
| MARFORCOM | Marine Corps Forces Command |

**Figure 2-1. Marine Air-Ground Task
Force Combat Camera Tasking Matrix.**

The MCIOC shall—

- Provide IO specific training to COMCAM personnel assigned to the MCIOC.
- Provide the MAGTF with guidance on the proper employment and use of COMCAM capabilities in support of IO.

See Marine Corps Warfighting Publication 3-40.4, *Marine Air-Ground Task Force Information Operations*, for additional information on IO.

SECRETARY OF THE NAVY RESPONSIBILITIES

The Secretary of the Navy shall ensure the availability of—

- COMCAM personnel with shipboard experience.
- Aircrew and diver-qualified COMCAM personnel with appropriate equipment to support operational requirements.
- MAGTF COMCAM personnel to support operational requirements.

DEFENSE IMAGERY MANAGEMENT OPERATIONS CENTER

The DIMOC provides the CJCS with current imagery transmitted from the Military Services involved in the ongoing operation or training exercise. The DIMOC is the central imagery reception point for all joint field documentation. It also distributes joint imagery to the Secretary of Defense and other local DOD users. In a joint operation, imagery must be transmitted to the DIMOC according to established DOD timelines. The DIMOC serves as the Pentagon's imagery resource center and provides all imagery received from field locations. Every image sent to the DIMOC has the potential to reach thousands of DOD and executive branch members.

There is no standing joint COMCAM management team; joint COMCAM management teams are task-organized for each joint contingency. Commanders involved in joint and multinational operations shall plan for, sustain, and employ COMCAM forces. Commanders shall expeditiously process and forward COMCAM imagery with captions to the DIMOC.

Chapter 3
Planning

A good COMCAM plan of employment significantly enhances the commander's decision-making process. Therefore, the COMCAM officer must—

- Understand the overall operation plan (OPLAN).

- Understand the commander's intent.

- Envision COMCAM's role and how to exploit COMCAM assets in support of the commander's intent.

- Understand the value, composition, and life cycle of imagery.

- Be involved in the planning process at all times and at all levels from the earliest possible moment.

LEVELS OF WAR

Combat camera is critical to the ability of the MAGTF to accomplish its mission at all levels of war. This is especially true because the global information environment spans the strategic, operational, and tactical levels of war. The operational aim for COMCAM is to acquire and disseminate COMCAM products to the MAGTF commander, his planners and staff, and higher headquarters. As with combat operations, speed and concentration of effort are paramount to operational planners; therefore, COMCAM products that support mission planning and identify critical information (such as convoy routes, danger zones, or ingress and egress routes) must be received in a timely and expedious manner. Commanders have a responsibility to include COMCAM as they conduct operations. Imagery supports command and control and enhances IO initiatives and strategic communication requirements. It can also be key in maintaining public support. Combat camera footage is often the only imagery of key events. This can significantly enhance media exposure.

The impact that emerging technologies and the evolving global media environment will have on all aspects of future military operations is difficult to fully anticipate or grasp. One thing is certain: information will become exponentially more abundant and potentially overwhelming. The MAGTF's COMCAM can be a force multiplier by supporting key objectives, providing accurate, easy-to-use imagery and printed or digital products, and providing these products to commanders based on a clear understanding of priorities and requirements. Commanders must realize that the information they control at the tactical level is the most time sensitive and must be used while valuable. This requires an aggressive acquisition and dissemination plan. Imagery not seen is imagery wasted; the first imagery seen is generally the most believed by global audiences. Commander's need to understand that battles are fought on the physical battlefield as well as on the Global Information Grid. Accurate, believable imagery will support mission IO objectives and strategic themes and messages.

COMBAT CAMERA OFFICER'S ROLE

Commanding officers with COMCAM assets will designate a COMCAM officer or director with releasing authority for all COMCAM products per MCO 3104.1A. The COMCAM officers cannot release imagery outside of the tasking command without the commander's written authorization. The COMCAM officer cannot release imagery to the public directly. This generally falls under the PA officer's duties. The commander designates the command's releasing authority.

Communication—internal and external—must be constantly monitored and adjusted. The COMCAM officer must consider multiple customers, competing timelines, long-term usefulness, and specific customer requirements. For instance, while supporting an ISR mission, the COMCAM officer should consider targets for the brigade or higher intelligence staff officer (G-2) or battalion or brigade intelligence staff officer (S-2). During an Operation Restore Hope, a single visual reconnaissance flight produced imagery for target folders, direct action missions, force protection, and convoy planners. It was used later to brief follow-on forces.

The COMCAM officer should also understand that commanders and their staffs rely on them to use COMCAM as a—

- Critical information provider.
- Force multiplier.
- Aid to force protection efforts.
- Situational awareness tool.
- Training critique tool.

The COMCAM officer must do more than simply produce photographs. He must provide meaningful images that are objective, thorough, accurate, timely, relevant, ready for use, and easy for customers to understand. This may require—

- An overlay with key information.
- A quickly edited video clip of a route reconnaissance.
- A Web-based imagery archive for use by planners, briefers, or analysts.

The COMCAM officer must understand the importance of tactical intelligence, which is the level of intelligence Marines need, generate, and use most often. The COMCAM officer should find ways to support the formulation of the commander's estimate of the situation, such as—

- Provide as accurate an image of the hostile situation as possible.

- Aid in situation development.

- Develop IO products.

- Provide support to force protection.

- Support targeting and combat assessment; e.g., battle damage assessment.

EARLY DEPLOYMENT

Personnel in support of COMCAM must deploy early to support various potential customers. Imagery of areas and facilities during initial site surveys can help advanced echelon forces plan logistical requirements. Imagery of approach lanes and landing zones can familiarize pilots and aircrews with terrain features and obstacles they may encounter. Imagery can help commanders visually describe the tactical situation to higher headquarters. Analysts need to see imagery of certain target areas, which over time, provide long-term insight to evolving situations. Historians usually want to see before and after imagery and detailed aspects of the Marines' environment (living conditions, fighting holes, weapons carriage, terrain, chow, or mail).

OPERATION PLANS AND OPERATION ORDERS

Combat camera must be included in OPLANs and OPORDs based on projected tasking and focus of effort. The COMCAM Marines must train with their assigned units and be included in the units' OPLANs and OPORDs. Guidance for conducting COMCAM operations comes from several sources. The standard contingency documentation plan (SCDP) establishes procedures, at the national level, for documenting military operations. This documentation normally supports COMCAM requirements. Tasking is referred to as programmed requirements. Deploying COMCAM teams will use the SCDP as a guide until the theater COMCAM representative provides further guidance, which is based on the theater commander's needs and the combat situation. The SCDP addresses documentation of combat and combat support operations. From this information, deploying COMCAM teams must be able to adapt COMCAM operations to almost any similar situation.

At the theater level, the combatant commander issues plans and orders to establish a joint COMCAM management team or other COMCAM guidance. Combat camera plans and orders are prepared by the COMCAM officer and appear as Appendix 9 (COMCAM) to Annex C (Operations) to the OPORD (see app. A for additional information). A COMCAM plan is required when preparing for exercises, operations, or routinely planned events. Combat camera planning will be carried out concurrently with operational planning. With minor modifications, Appendix 9 can also be used by the command to form the COMCAM plan for garrison use.

COMBAT CAMERA PRODUCTS USAGE

The value of COMCAM products is based on a combination of timeliness and content. Timely COMCAM products act as force multipliers. During Operation Iraqi Freedom, Marine Corps COMCAM teams documented actions in the cities of the of Al Anbar province. These images were made available daily through an online searchable database and, within hours, utilized by IO officers, planners, and commanders to plan for current operations and the development of IO/PSYOP products. Additionally, the aggregate of imagery was used to show progress in the streets of Al Anbar from 2005 to 2008, also known as the "Awakening." The imagery collected provided valid information for commanders, staffs, and planners to prepare their units for the upcoming conflict and foster a greater understanding of the areas of operation their units would be operating in. Additionally, imagery was provided to worldwide news agencies as the "first imagery," many times providing visual proof to stories and at times dispelling our adversary's misinformation. Historically, significant imagery is archived as a permanent record of what occurred at a specific time and place. Compelling, historical imagery has repeatedly been used to champion the Marine Corps' existence or need for resources. Failure to use COMCAM in training and operations will result in a lack of historical imagery.

WHO USES COMBAT CAMERA PRODUCTS?

Combat camera products directly or indirectly support the warfighter whether planning the next operation, being used for a brief at HQMC or higher, and a myriad of functions in between.

Combat camera imagery from World War II, Vietnam, and Iraq, which was originally gathered to support a commander's imagery requirements, is repeatedly used to produce training manuals, lessons learned, historical programs, and Commandant of the Marine Corps-produced motivational videos or recruiting posters. Understanding the varied multitude of personnel who use COMCAM products and the uses of these products help planners determine equipment requirements and the best mix of COMCAM assets, required to document any event.

The DODI 5040.04 requires the Services to provide imagery of current operations to the DOD; these images are eventually routed to the National Archives in Washington, DC. Combat camera imagery is routinely used to support a multitude of individuals or organizations simultaneously; e.g., the on-scene commander, the CJCS, joint COMCAM efforts, planners, analysts, civil affairs personnel, engineers, military police, and PA efforts.

As society becomes more visually oriented in communications, the demand for timely imagery will increase and a wider variety of personnel will need to access the same COMCAM products for support. Therefore, commanders must make COMCAM products available and useful to as many users and planners as possible. With the quantity of information available at any one time, the value of quality information has grown tremendously. Combat camera provides commanders with a directed imagery acquisition and production capability that is comparable to any civilian imagery professional.

Chapter 4
Operations

A principal aim of command and control is to enhance the commander's ability to make sound and timely decisions. Quality information adds value to the decisionmaking process and is critical to the success or failure of an operation. Therefore, the commander must determine his information requirements and ensure that information is managed effectively. Combat camera assists the MAGTF commander in the decisionmaking process by making a major contribution to the understanding of the battlespace and the threat. Combat camera should also be an integral element of the decisionmaking process through which the commander implements decisions. The COMCAM Marines also need to know the mission, tactical situation, tasks to be accomplished, support available, and the communications required to accomplish the mission.

MISSION REQUIREMENTS

Combat camera products support various mission requirements simultaneously. Combat camera officers train with commanders and staffs and develop relationships during planning and exercises. These established working relationships produce streamlined communication, anticipation of a commander's requirements, and fine-tuned COMCAM support. Throughout the MAGTF, COMCAM is organized to support the COMCAM requirements of the warfighter. Tasking for COMCAM support can come from the combatant commander, on-scene commander, local commander, or personnel within the chain of command.

Combat camera is an integral feature of the MAGTF and its operations and should not be considered an independent entity. Combat camera missions are in direct support of the commander's critical information requirements and provide products that assist in gaining the advantage against the enemy. Through the specialized assets that COMCAM brings to the commander, it supports the many different missions of the MAGTF to include—

- IO.
- Strategic communication.
- Civil-military operations (CMO).
- Foreign humanitarian assistance and disaster relief.
- Counterdrug operations.
- Peacekeeping operations.
- PSYOP.
- Intelligence and counterintelligence.
- PA.
- Training.

Information Operations

Decisionmakers use IO to affect adversary information and information systems while defending their own information and information systems (see fig. 4-1). The force that best controls, shapes, and safeguards information and information systems will enjoy a decided military advantage. Information operations interact with the global information environment and exploit or deny the adversary's information and decision capabilities. Units conduct IO across the full range of military operations. Information operations continue beyond the end of hostilities and into the pacification and nation-building phase.

Figure 4-1. Information Operations.

Strategic Communication

Strategic communication is defined as focused [US] Government efforts to understand and engage key audiences to create, strengthen, or preserve conditions favorable for the advancement of [US] Government interests, policies, and objectives through the use of coordinated programs, plans, themes, messages, and products synchronized with the actions of all instruments of national power (Joint Publication 1-02, *Department of Defense Dictionary of Military and Associated Terms*). Combat camera supports strategic communications by providing imagery incorporated into strategic communication themes and messages, images depicting all US Government efforts, and still and video evidence of military engagements of counter adversaries that cause civilian casualties. Combat camera imagery and printed materials may also be used to support CMO and PSYOP efforts to inform the populous of US Government efforts to minimize civilian casualties, employ appropriate rules of engagement to minimize civilian casualties, and to help support awareness of the effects that cause civilian casualties.

Civil-Military Operations

Civil-military operations activities encompass the relationship between military forces, civil authorities, and people in a friendly or foreign country or area (see fig. 4-2). They support national policy and implement US national objectives by coordinating with, influencing, developing, or controlling indigenous infra-structures in operational areas. Civil-military operations secure local acceptance of and support for US forces. Civil-military operations are important for gaining information dominance because of its ability to interface with key organizations and individuals in the global information environment; e.g., CMO's traditional relationship with nongovernmental organizations and international organizations. Combat camera can influence ideas, concepts, and issues via printed fliers, photographs, video productions, or Web-based graphics.

Foreign Humanitarian Assistance and Disaster Relief

Combat camera is an invaluable asset during foreign humanitarian assistance missions, not only as a tool to document US efforts to aid countries hit by natural and manmade disasters, but also as an aid to IO efforts (see fig. 4-3 on page 4-6). Combat camera Marines assigned to a MEU can provide time-sensitive imagery to on-scene commanders and higher commands during noncombatant evacuation operations.

Figure 4-2. Civil-Military Operations.

Combat camera can be attached to the civil engineer battalion to document conditions before and after civil engineer battalion operations, capturing the improvements in living conditions and foreign humanitarian assistance provided during operations.

Imagery collected by COMCAM assets can also be used to determine levels of destruction in the event of natural disasters.

Counterdrug Operations

Many factors are unique to counterdrug operations, such as a high degree of interagency and international coordination. Most significantly, the legal and law enforcement aspects are extremely sensitive. Commanders use COMCAM imagery to familiarize their Marines with terrain features, show facilities for use in planning command posts, document seizures and evidence, and protect US forces from legal reprisal.

**Figure 4-3. Foreign Humanitarian
Assistance and Disaster Relief.**

Peacekeeping Operations

Because of the nature of peacekeeping operations, COMCAM is often the only means to provide imagery to higher headquarters and the press (see fig. 4-4). Imagery collected can provide proof of military involvement if and when false accusations are presented. Imagery collected can also demonstrate the successes involved during peacekeeping operations. These images can enhance the commander's decisionmaking process and maintain public support for the mission.

Psychological Operations

One of the five pillars of IO is PSYOP. Combat camera is an invaluable resource to support efforts to shape the battlefield and execute a PSYOP campaign plan. Psychological operations are planned operations that convey selected information and indicators to foreign audiences to influence their emotions; motives; objective reasoning; and, ultimately, the behavior of foreign governments, organizations, groups, and individuals. A

Figure 4-4. Peacekeeping Operations.

major element of PSYOP is propaganda, which is any form of communication in support of national objectives designed to influence the opinions, emotions, attitudes, or behavior of any group to benefit the sponsor either directly or indirectly.

Intelligence and Counterintelligence

Combat camera supports the commander's intelligence and counterintelligence requirements by providing COMCAM products to support the following actions:

- Identify and evaluate existing conditions and capabilities.
- Aid in identifying friendly critical vulnerabilities.
- Assist in developing and evaluating friendly courses of action.
- Enhance tempo through effective information flow, taking advantage of all available communication means to disseminate imagery.

Public Affairs

Public affairs informs and educates the target audience whether it is within the Marine Corps or part of the general public (see fig. 4-5). Public affairs influence is a by-product—the result or effects of people being informed—rather than the design or intent of the communication. Combat camera can support PA missions with graphics, photography, video products, and digital and printed media. Public affairs credibility is based on truthfulness. Combat camera is not a function of PA, but a separate discipline and entity that can support PA requirements.

Figure 4-5. Public Affairs.

Training

Training is a professional and moral imperative (see fig. 4-6 on page 4-10). It is the Marine leader's responsibility to ensure that his Marines are properly trained and prepared for combat. Combat camera provides products that facilitate the leader's evaluation of the effectiveness of the training package and whether or not the training objectives have been met. Safety is a major concern during the training process. Combat camera products can assist in identifying unsafe conditions or procedures. Combat camera can also provide materials to be used for training evolutions in the form of video and still imagery assets and/or printed materials.

Figure 4-6. Training.

JOINT COMBAT CAMERA REQUIREMENTS

Combat camera forces are tasked, deployed, and employed as an integral part of joint/combined and multinational operations to ensure documentation of the entire scope of US military activities and DOD components during wartime operations, worldwide crises, contingencies, joint exercises, and other events of significant national interest.

Combat camera is an operational mission assigned to the J-3 [operations directorate of a joint staff]. The joint force information operations chief (J-39) is responsible for COMCAM activities. The J-39 generates COMCAM mission assignment tasking and receives mission assignments from higher authority and within the joint task force. The J-39 will establish priorities and coordinate support for COMCAM missions with requesting commanders within the joint force. It is important that the joint COMCAM team's officer in charge work to keep the J-39 informed of all COMCAM activities. The COMCAM operation in support of the joint force's plan expands beyond the role of the IO plan. When Marine Corps commands are the lead for joint or combined task forces, the Marine Corps commander will assign a COMCAM officer to be the joint combat camera management team officer in charge.

Chapter 5
Systems and Equipment

Marine Corps operational COMCAM capabilities provide the MAGTF commander direct support in the form of photography, videography, graphic products, and lithography. Teams use organic Marine Corps communications systems to disseminate COMCAM both horizontally and vertically throughout the MAGTF. The MAGTF COMCAM systems produce products that interoperate with joint imagery requirements.

INDIVIDUAL ACQUISITION SYSTEMS

The MAGTF's COMCAM personnel deploy with equipment and systems capable of all-weather, day and night digital imagery acquisition. These systems are MOS-specific and include still and video digital cameras, limited printing and video duplications, night vision, and communications equipment provided by the communications section.

TACTICAL IMAGERY PRODUCTION SYSTEM

The tactical imagery production system (TIPS) is a self-contained, deployable production unit designed for use by COMCAM teams. It provides high volume visual information, production, reproduction, and transmission in direct support of the MAGTF commander. The TIPS is deployed and employed at major subordinate commands or higher levels within the MAGTF.

During Operations Iraqi Freedom and Enduring Freedom, TIPS was used as a direct support asset to the MAGTF commander and major subordinate commands.

COMMUNICATIONS REQUIREMENTS

Communications capabilities must be seamless. Imagery collected on the battlefield may be accessible to operational planners, with a justifiable requirement for ongoing imagery collection and IO, regardless of location. Combat camera communications requirements must be integrated into organic Marine Corps communications systems and interface with all current and future imagery production systems.

Communications connectivity requirements center on interoperability with the MAGTF's organic tactical data network. It is imperative that the COMCAM officer work closely with the MAGTF communications staff to ensure connectivity requirements are met with as little impact as possible on the network. The COMCAM mission to disseminate imagery is vital, but should never degrade the tactical data network. The TIPS and other COMCAM systems are organic to the MAGTF, but should be managed to ensure the commander's critical information requirements are supported, not hindered.

Appendix A
Sample Appendix 9
(COMCAM) to Annex C (Operations)

CLASSIFICATION

Copy no. __ of __ copies
OFFICIAL DESIGNATION
OF COMMAND
PLACE OF ISSUE
Date-time group
Message reference number

APPENDIX 9 (COMBAT CAMERA) TO ANNEX C
(OPERATIONS) TO OPERATION ORDER (NUMBER) (U)

(U) REFERENCES:

    (a) Regulations
    (b) Required maps and charts
    (c) Other relevant documents

(U) TIME ZONE:

1. (U) <u>Situation</u>. This paragraph includes a brief general description of the situation; i.e., information and COMCAM support that paragraph 1 of the OPLAN does not cover and the intended purpose of this appendix.

Page number

CLASSIFICATION

CLASSIFICATION

a. (U) <u>Friendly Forces</u>. Outline the higher headquarters' plan, the COMCAM annex, and adjacent unit COMCAM plans. Provide information on friendly coalition forces that may affect the COMCAM mission. Note COMCAM resources supporting the unit.

b. (U) <u>Attachments and Detachments</u>. Identify all augmenting COMCAM units supporting this command and all attached/assigned subordinate units. Include effective dates, if applicable.

c. (U) <u>Enemy Forces</u>. List information on the threat force, its relationship to COMCAM mission, and any information not included in the OPLAN/OPORD that may affect the COMCAM mission.

d. (U) <u>Assumptions</u>. List any additional assumptions or information not included in the general situation that will affect the COMCAM mission. Include a communications appraisal of tactical imagery transmission requirements.

2. (U) <u>Mission</u>. There must be a clear, concise statement of the COMCAM mission. This statement should reflect the broad COMCAM mission during the particular operation or event, not the overall military mission. Communications goals should be clearly stated in appropriate detail. For a plan that supports combat operations, a determination should be made for direct support, general support, and priority of support.

Page number

CLASSIFICATION

CLASSIFICATION

3. (U) <u>Execution</u>. This paragraph provides a summary of the overall intended course of action.

a. (U) <u>Concept of Operation</u>. Briefly summarize the COMCAM OPLAN, include COMCAM imagery and printing priorities.

b. (U) <u>Tasks</u>. Identify and assign supporting tasks to each COMCAM element of subordinate and supporting units. Route tasks through the G-3 or S-3 as appropriate.

c. (U) <u>Coordinating Instructions</u>. Provisions for combat documentation shall be included in the plan. Include support provisions for COMCAM teams, priorities, and other instructions. Give details on coordination, task organization, and groupings. List instructions that apply to two or more subordinate elements or units. Include all details in direct support of commanders, operators, analysts, and other customers; details on embarkation schedules, any restrictions because of weight or equipment, imagery transmission and dissemination plans; or any other details.

4. (U) <u>Service Support</u>. Service support includes statements of administrative and logistical arrangements.

a. (U) <u>Administration</u>. Provide a statement of the administrative arrangements applicable to this operation. If they are long or not ready for inclusion in the OPLAN,

Page number

CLASSIFICATION

CLASSIFICATION

arrangements may be issued separately and referenced there. Release authority will be named in annex F (Public Affairs). Refer to it accordingly. Special consideration should be given to the chain of custody of imagery with evidential value; e.g., imagery of war crimes, atrocities against civilians.

b. (U) Logistics. Provide a statement of the logistical arrangements applicable to this operation. Specific coordination should be included, if possible, but arrangements may be issued separately and referenced there if they are too long.

5. (U) Command and Signal. List signal, visual imaging, and satellite communications policies; headquarters/joint COMCAM team and military media center locations or movements; and code words, code names, and liaison elements.

ACKNOWLEDGE RECEIPT

Name
Rank and Service
Title

Page number

CLASSIFICATION

Appendix B
Sample Concept of Employment

Marine air-ground task force commanders are free to distribute COMCAM assets as they see fit. However, to provide them with as much flexibility as possible, the following concept of employment has been developed.

MAGTF AND MAJOR
SUBORDINATE COMMAND COMCAM TASKS

- Manage and coordinate imagery taskings with GCE, ACE, and Marine logistics group (formerly force service support group) COMCAM assets throughout the MEF/MEB area of operations.

- Dispatch, as needed, MEF/MEB COMCAM teams to events of interest for the tactical, operational, and strategic decisionmaking processes for the CE and to support the IO campaign plan.

- Use available communications assets to transmit imagery vertically from the major subordinate commands to higher headquarters and horizontally from adjacent and coalition commands.

- Provide reliable archival capability of imagery for use in briefings and command chronological records for situation assessments and after action information.

- Provide rapid reproduction of various media formats for information dissemination.

PROPOSED TABLES

The MEF/MEB CE, GCE, ACE, Marine logistics group, radar control terminal, and MEU will provide imagery of interest to CEs and higher commands to support the tactical, operational, and strategic decisionmaking processes. For all of these units, table or organization (T/O) personnel have organic still and video acquisition gear and ruggedized laptops with transmission capability. The TIPS contains imagery acquisition, transmission, and print/production capabilities; is mobile and self-powered; and can displace rapidly.

Note: The MEU does not have a resident TIPS capability.

No current T/E for a MEF COMCAM team exists. The current T/O only supports a captain 4602 MOS. Personnel assets required to support the MEF CE will have to come from organic COMCAM assets in the MEF or globally sourced through the respective Marine Corps forces.

**Marine Expeditionary Force/Marine
Expeditionary Brigade Command Element**

Personnel:
1 to 8 (task-organized)

1 COMCAM officer (CWO/Capt)
1 COMCAM chief (GySgt/MSgt)
2 combat photographers (Cpl/LCpl)
2 combat videographers (Cpl/LCpl)
2 combat production specialists (Cpl/LCpl)
1 combat (Cpl/LCpl)

Equipment:
2 digital still imagery kits
2 video imagery kits
2 acquisition/transmission kits
1 TIPS

Initial consumable stock of 180 days

2HMMWVs

Legend:
Capt	captain
Cpl	corporal
CWO	chief warrant officer
GySgt	gunnery sergeant
HMMWV	high mobility multipurpose wheeled vehicle
LCpl	lance corporal
MSgt	master sergeant

Ground Combat Element

Personnel:
1 to 13 (organic assets)

1 COMCAM officer
1 COMCAM operations chief (MSgt/GySgt)
3 combat photographers (Sgt/Cpl)
3 combat videographers (Sgt/Cpl)
4 combat production specialists (Cpl/LCpl)

Equipment:
Requisite T/E equipment per listed T/O
1 TIPS

Consumable stock for 60 days

Initial consumable stock of 180 days

2 HMMWVs

Legend:
Cpl	corporal
GySgt	gunnery sergeant
HMMWV	high mobility multipurpose wheeled vehicle
LCpl	lance corporal
MSgt	master sergeant
Sgt	sergeant

Aviation Combat Element

Personnel:
1 to 7 (organic assets)

1 COMCAM officer (CWO)
1 COMCAM operations chief (GySgt/SSgt)
2 combat photographers (Cpl/LCpl)
2 combat videographers (Cpl/LCpl)
2 combat production specialists (Cpl/LCpl)

Equipment:
Initial consumable stock of 180 days

2 HMMWVs

Requisite T/E equipment per listed T/O

Consumable stock for 60 days

Legend:
Cpl	corporal
CWO	chief warrant officer
GySgt	gunnery sergeant
HMMWV	high mobility multipurpose wheeled vehicle
LCpl	lance corporal
SSgt	staff sergeant

Marine Logistics Group

Personnel:
1 to 5 (organic assets)

1 COMCAM operations chief (GySgt/SSgt)
2 combat photographers (Cpl/LCpl)
1 combat videographer (Cpl/LCpl)
1 combat production specialist (Cpl/LCpl)

Equipment:
Requisite T/E equipment per listed T/O

Consumable stock for 60 days

Initial consumable stock of 180 days

2 HMMWVs

Legend:
Cpl	corporal
GySgt	gunnery sergeant
HMMWV	high mobility multipurpose wheeled vehicle
LCpl	lance corporal
SSgt	staff sergeant

Regimental Combat Teams

Personnel:
1 to 6 (task-organized)

1 COMCAM operations chief (GySgt/SSgt)
2 combat photographers (Sgt/Cpl)
2 combat videographer (Sgt/Cpl)
1 combat production specialist (Cpl/LCpl)

Equipment:
Requisite T/E equipment per listed T/O

Consumable stock for 60 days

Initial consumable stock of 180 days

Legend:
Cpl   corporal
GySgt   gunnery sergeant
LCpl   lance corporal
SSgt   staff sergeant
Sgt   sergeant

Marine Expeditionary Unit

Personnel:
1 to 3 (organic assets)

1 COMCAM operations chief (GySgt/SSgt)
1 combat photographer (Cpl/LCpl)
1 combat videographer (Cpl/LCpl) no T/O

Equipment:
Requisite T/E equipment per listed T/O

Consumable stock for 60 days

Initial consumable stock of 180 days

2 HMMWVs

Legend:
Cpl	corporal
GySgt	gunnery sergeant
HMMWV	high mobility multipurpose wheeled vehicle
LCpl	lance corporal
SSgt	staff sergeant

Appendix C
Training

Combat camera personnel apply the training principles of—

- The building block approach.
- Focus on expected combat missions.
- Focus on unit core capabilities and individual core skills.
- Organization of tasks into executable events.
- Sustainment of training.

These principles are key to successful training during peacetime and in combat. As an integral part of the MAGTF commander's decisionmaking process, COMCAM personnel must train to enhance individual skills learned at formal schools and to become combat-ready as units and teams. The NAVMC 3500.26 provides a centralized repository of training requirements for OccFld 4600, allowing for the development of continuous and progressive training accomplished by individual, team, and collective training.

INDIVIDUAL AND INITIAL TEAM TRAINING

Currently all OccFld 4600 formal school instruction is conducted at Defense Information School. Marine COMCAM personnel receive core training in individual skills for MOS qualification. Initial team training is accomplished on the TIPS, preparing Marines for operational COMCAM units.

TEAM TRAINING

Upon the arrival of COMCAM Marines at their assigned unit, they are assimilated into the existing UTP. The COMCAM officer and senior staff noncommissioned officer in charge follow NAVMC 3500.26, enhancing the individual and initial team training learned at Defense Information School. Individual and initial team training is further expanded based on the UTP and current mission requirements defined by the MAGTF commander.

COLLECTIVE TRAINING

Collective training is accomplished through the UTP. Because collective readiness and individual readiness are closely related, NAVMC 3500.26 contains individual and collective training events. Collective training encompasses those events that require two or more personnel for successful completion. The COMCAM officer develops the mission essential task list based on lists of higher headquarters.

Glossary

Section I: Acronyms and Abbreviations

ACE. . . . . .aviation combat element

CE . . . . .command element
CJCS . . . . .Chairman of the Joint Chiefs of Staff
CMO . . . . civil-military operations
COMCAM . . . . combat camera

DIMOC . . . . . .Defense Imagery Management Operations Center
DOD . . . . .Department of Defense
DODI. . . . . .Department of Defense instruction

G-2 . . . . brigade or higher intelligence staff officer
G-3 . . . . brigade or higher operations staff officer
GCE. . . . . ground combat element

HQMC. . . . . .Headquarters, Marine Corps

IO . . . . information operations
ISR . . . . intelligence, surveillance, and reconnaissance

J-39 . . . . information operations chief of a joint staff

LCE. . . . . logistics combat element

MAGTF. . . . . Marine air-ground task force
MCCDC . . . . . . Marine Corps Combat Development Command
MCIOC . . . . Marine Corps Information Operations Center
MCO . . . . .Marine Corps order

MCWP . . . . Marine Corps warfighting publication
MEB . . . . Marine expeditionary brigade
MEF . . . . Marine expeditionary force
MEU . . . . Marine expeditionary unit
MOS . . . . .military occupational specialty

NAVMC . . . . Navy/Marine Corps departmental publication

OccFld . . . . occupational field
OPLAN . . . . operation plan
OPORD . . . . operation order

PA . . . . .public affairs
PSYOP . . . . psychological operations

S-2 . . . . .battalion or brigade intelligence staff officer
(Army; Marine Corps battalion or regiment)
S-3 . . . . .battalion or brigade operations staff officer
(Army; Marine Corps battalion or regiment)
SCDP . . . . .standard contingency documentation plan

T/E . . . . table of equipment
TIPS . . . . tactical imagery production system
T/O . . . . .table of organization

US . . . . United States
UTP . . . . unit training plan

Section II. Definitions

area of operations—An operational area defined by the joint force commander for land and maritime forces. Areas of operation do not typically encompass the entire operational area of the joint force commander, but should be large enough for component commanders to accomplish their missions and protect their forces. (JP 1-02)

battle damage assessment—The estimate of damage resulting from the application of lethal or nonlethal military force. Battle damage assessment is composed of physical damage assessment, functional damage assessment, and target system assessment. (JP 1-02) The timely and accurate estimate of the damage resulting from the application of military force. Battle damage assessment estimates physical damage to a particular target, functional damage to that target, and the capability of the entire target system to continue its operations. (MCRP 5-12C)

battlespace—All aspects of air, surface, subsurface, land, space, and electromagnetic spectrum which encompass the area of influence and area of interest. (MCRP 5-12C)

civil-military operations—The activities of a commander that establish, maintain, influence, or exploit relations between military forces, governmental and nongovernmental civilian organizations and authorities, and the civilian populace in a friendly, neutral, or hostile operational area in order to facilitate military operations, to consolidate and achieve operational US objectives. Civil-military operations may include performance by military forces of activities and functions normally the responsibility of the local, regional, or national government. These activities may occur prior to, during, or subsequent to other military actions.

They may also occur, if directed, in the absence of other military operations. Civil-military operations may be performed by designated civil affairs, by other military forces, or by a combination of civil affairs and other forces. Also called **CMO**. (JP 1-02)

combat camera—The acquisition and utilization of still and motion imagery in support of operational and planning requirements across the range of military operations and during exercises. Also called **COMCAM**. (MCRP 5-12C)

combined operation—An operation conducted by forces of two or more Allied nations acting together for the accomplishment of a single mission. (JP 1-02)

command and control—The exercise of authority and direction by a properly designated commander over assigned and attached forces in the accomplishment of the mission. Command and control functions are performed through an arrangement of personnel, equipment, communications, facilities, and procedures employed by a commander in planning, directing, coordinating, and controlling forces and operations in the accomplishment of the mission. (JP 1-02) The means by which a commander recognizes what needs to be done and sees to it that appropriate actions are taken. (MCRP 5-12C)

commander's intent—A concise expression of the purpose of the operation and the desired end state. It may also include the commander's assessment of the adversary commander's intent and an assessment of where and how much risk is acceptable during the operation. (JP 1-02)

component—1. One of the subordinate organizations that constitute a joint force. Normally a joint force is organized with a combination of Service and functional components. (JP 1-02, part 1 of a 2 part definition)

coordination—The action necessary to ensure adequately integrated relationships between separate organizations located in the same area. Coordination may include such matters as fire support, emergency defense measures, area intelligence, and other situations in which coordination is considered necessary. (MCRP 5-12C)

counterintelligence—Information gathered and activities conducted to protect against espionage, other intelligence activities, sabotage, or assassinations conducted by or on behalf of foreign governments or elements thereof, foreign organizations, or foreign persons, or international terrorist activities. (JP 1-02) The active and passive measures intended to deny the enemy valuable information about the friendly situation, to detect and neutralize hostile intelligence collection, and to deceive the enemy as to friendly capabilities and intentions. (MCRP 5-12C)

dissemination—Conveyance of intelligence to users in a suitable form. (MCRP 5-12C)

force protection—Preventive measures taken to mitigate hostile actions against Department of Defense personnel (to include family members), resources, facilities, and critical information. Force protection does not include actions to defeat the enemy or protect against accidents, weather, or disease. (JP 1-02)

foreign humanitarian assistance—Department of Defense activities, normally in support of the United States Agency for International Development or Department of State conducted outside the United States, its territories, and possessions to relieve or reduce human suffering, disease, hunger, or privation. (JP 1-02)

general support—1. That support which is given to the supported force as a whole and not to any particular subdivision thereof. (JP 1-02, part 1 of a 2-part definition)

helicopter landing zone—A specified ground area for landing assault helicopters to embark or disembark troops and/or cargo. A landing zone may contain one or more landing sites. (JP 1-02)

intelligence—1. The product resulting from the collection, processing, integration, evaluation, analysis, and interpretation of available information concerning foreign nations, hostile or potentially hostile forces or elements, or areas of actual or potential operations. The term is also applied to the activity which results in the product and to the organizations engaged in such activity. (JP 1-02) Knowledge about the enemy or the surrounding environment needed to support decisionmaking. This knowledge is the result of the collection, processing, exploitation, evaluation, integration, analysis, and interpretation of available information about the battlespace and threat. (MCRP 5-12C)

intelligence, surveillance and reconnaissance—An activity that synchronizes and integrates the planning and operation of sensors, assets, and processing, exploitation, and dissemination systems in direct support of current and future operations. This is an integrated intelligence and operations function. Also called ISR. (JP 1-02).

joint force—A general term applied to a force composed of significant elements, assigned or attached, of two or more Military Departments operating under a single joint force commander. (JP 1-02).

joint operations—A general term to describe military actions conducted by joint forces or by Service forces in relationships (e.g., support, coordinating authority), which, of themselves, do not create joint forces. (JP 1-02)

joint task force—A joint force that is constituted and so designated by the Secretary of Defense, a combatant commander, a subunified commander, or an existing joint task force commander. Also called **JTF**. (JP 1-02)

multinational operations—A collective term to describe military actions conducted by forces of two or more nations, usually undertaken within the structure of a coalition or alliance. (JP 1-02)

psychological operations—Planned operations to convey selected information and indicators to foreign audiences to influence their emotions, motives, objective reasoning, and ultimately the behavior of foreign governments, organizations, groups, and individuals. The purpose of psychological operations is to induce or reinforce foreign attitudes and behavior favorable to the originator's objectives. Also called **PSYOP**. (JP 1-02)

public affairs—Those public information, command information, and community relations activities directed toward both the external and internal publics with interest in the Department of Defense. Also called **PA**. (JP 1-02)

situational awareness—Knowledge and understanding of the current situation that promotes timely, relevant, and accurate assessment of friendly, enemy, and other operations within the battlespace in order to facilitate decisionmaking. An informational perspective and skill that foster an ability to determine quickly the context and relevance of events that are unfolding. Also called **SA**. (MCRP 5-12C)

strategic communication—Focused United States Government efforts to understand andengage key audiences to create, strengthen, or preserve conditions favorable for the advancement of United States Government interests, policies, and objectives through the use of coordinated programs, plans, themes, messages, and products synchronized with the actions of all instruments of national power. (JP 5-0)

tactical intelligence—Intelligence required for planning and conduct of tactical operations. (JP 1-02) Intelligence concerned primary with the location, capabilities, and possible intentions of enemy units on the battlefield and the tactical aspects of terrain and weather within the battlespace. (MCRP 5-12C)

target—1. An entity or object considered for possible engagement or other action. 2. In intelligence usage, a country, area, installation, agency, or person against which intelligence operations are directed. 3. An area designated and numbered for future firing. (JP 1-02, parts 1 through 3 of a 4-part definition)

visual information—Various visual media with or without sound. Generally, visual information includes still and motion photography, audio video recording, graphic arts, visual aids, models, display, and visual presentation. Also called **VI**. (JP 1-02)

References

Department of Defense Instructions (DODIs)
5040.02   Visual Information (VI)
5040.04   Joint Combat Camera (COMCAM) Program

Joint Publication (JP)
1-02   Department of Defense Dictionary of Military and
             Associated Terms

Navy/Marine Corps Departmental Publication (NAVMC)
3500.26   Combat Camera Training and Readiness Manual

Marine Corps Orders (MCOs)
3104.1A   Marine Corps Combat Camera Program
3120.10   Marine Corps Information Operations
             Program (MCIOP)

Marine Corps Warfighting Publication (MCWP)
3-40.4   Marine Air-Ground Task Force
             Information Operations

Marine Corps Reference Publication (MCRP)
3-0A   Unit Training Management Guide

www.ingramcontent.com/pod-product-compliance
Lightning Source LLC
Chambersburg PA
CBHW070607290526
45790CB00002B/821

* 9 7 8 1 4 9 0 5 6 1 2 8 8 *